Food List

For

Prediabetes

Jerry V. Hatcher

Table of Contents

Introduction:

Understanding Prediabetes

In a world where our lifestyles are becoming increasingly sedentary and our diets often consist of convenient, but not necessarily nutritious, choices, the prevalence of prediabetes is on the rise. Prediabetes is a wake-up call, an early warning sign that our bodies are struggling to regulate blood sugar levels effectively. It's a crucial juncture, a fork in the road where we have the power to make informed choices that can significantly impact our health trajectory.

Welcome to "Food List for Prediabetes." In the following pages, we'll embark on a journey of empowerment, education, and transformation. This book is designed as your companion, offering insights, strategies, and a comprehensive food list to help you navigate the realm of prediabetes management through a well-balanced diet.

The journey toward better health isn't about deprivation; it's about choice. Choice to fuel your body with foods that nourish and sustain. Choice to embrace a lifestyle that supports your well-being. Choice to take control of your health narrative and rewrite it in a way that fosters vitality and longevity.

Throughout this book, we'll explore the intricacies of prediabetes, unravel the connection between diet and blood sugar management, and delve into the vast realm of prediabetes-friendly foods. You'll discover the power of a balanced plate and how to construct meals that promote stable blood sugar levels, while still being delicious and satisfying.

But this book is not just about lists and meal plans. It's about understanding the why behind your food choices. It's about making informed decisions that align with your health goals and aspirations. It's about recognizing that you hold the reins of your wellness journey, and armed with the right knowledge, you can steer yourself toward a brighter, healthier future.

So, whether you're newly diagnosed with prediabetes, seeking preventive measures, or supporting a loved one on this path, "Food List for Prediabetes" is here to guide you. As you turn the pages and absorb the information within, remember that each choice you make, each meal you craft, is an opportunity to pave the way for a life lived with vitality and purpose. Let's embark on this transformative journey together.

Chapter 1

What is Prediabetes?

In the intricate landscape of health and wellness, prediabetes stands as a critical crossroads. It's a condition that precedes type 2 diabetes, a harbinger of potential challenges, yet also an invitation to proactive change. In this chapter, we will delve into the depths of prediabetes, illuminating its definition, shedding light on its risk factors, and emphasizing the significance of early intervention.

Defining Prediabetes: The Gray Zone

Prediabetes is the intermediate phase between normal blood sugar levels and the elevated levels characteristic of diabetes. Often referred to as the "gray zone," prediabetes is a signal that your body's intricate blood sugar regulation mechanism is faltering. While you may not yet meet the diagnostic criteria for diabetes, the warning signs are evident, demanding attention and action.

Recognizing the Red Flags: Risk Factors and Signs

Understanding the risk factors associated with prediabetes is akin to deciphering a code to unlock potential health challenges. These risk factors include obesity, a sedentary lifestyle, and a family history of diabetes, high blood pressure, and age— particularly for those over 45. Additionally, certain ethnic backgrounds, such as African American, Hispanic, Native American, and Asian American, are more susceptible.

While prediabetes often operates incognito, it does offer subtle signs that warrant vigilance. Increased thirst, frequent urination, unexplained fatigue, and blurred vision are signals that your body may be struggling to regulate blood sugar levels. Heeding these signs and understanding the role of prediabetes in your overall health can empower you to take proactive steps toward a healthier future.

The Power of Early Intervention: A Fork in the Road

Prediabetes should not be underestimated. It's a crossroads where you can either continue along the path of potential health complications or make a U-turn toward a different destination. The choices you make at this junction can alter the course of your health journey. By acknowledging prediabetes as an opportunity for early intervention, you set the stage for impactful changes that can mitigate the progression to type 2 diabetes.

The journey ahead is one of education, empowerment, and informed decision-making. As we navigate the chapters to come, remember that prediabetes is not a life sentence but a call to action. It's a chapter in your health narrative that you have the power to rewrite, armed with knowledge and determination. Let's move forward together, exploring the role of diet in managing prediabetes and laying the foundation for a healthier and more vibrant life.

Chapter 3:

Prediabetes-Friendly Foods

In the intricate tapestry of managing prediabetes, the foods you choose become the threads that weave the fabric of your well-being. This chapter is your guide to a palette of nourishment – a compilation of prediabetes-friendly foods that can help stabilize your blood sugar levels, boost your energy, and foster your overall health.

Complex Carbohydrates: The Foundation of Sustenance

Complex carbohydrates are the cornerstone of a prediabetes-friendly diet. These nutrient-rich gems provide a steady stream of energy while minimizing the rapid spikes in blood sugar often associated with simple carbohydrates. Here's a selection of complex carbohydrate sources to consider incorporating into your meals:

- Whole grains: Quinoa, brown rice, whole wheat, oats, barley

- Legumes: Lentils, chickpeas, black beans, kidney beans

- Starchy vegetables: Sweet potatoes, yams, peas, corn

Lean Proteins: Building Blocks for Balance

Protein plays a vital role in managing prediabetes by promoting satiety, aiding in muscle repair, and stabilizing blood sugar levels. Opt for lean protein sources that bring a wealth of nutrients without excessive saturated fats:

- Poultry: Skinless chicken, turkey

- Fish: Salmon, tuna, trout

- Plant-based proteins: Tofu, tempeh, legumes, nuts, seeds

Healthy Fats: Fueling Your Body Wisely

Fats are not the enemy; they are an essential part of a balanced diet. Embrace heart-healthy fats that contribute to improved insulin sensitivity and overall well-being:

- Avocado

- Nuts: Almonds, walnuts, pistachios

- Seeds: Chia seeds, flaxseeds

- Olive oil

High-Fiber Foods: Nature's Digestive Allies

Fiber is a superhero in the world of prediabetes management. It slows down the absorption of sugar and helps maintain steady blood sugar levels. Here are fiber-rich foods to include:

- Non-starchy vegetables: Leafy greens, broccoli, cauliflower, bell peppers

- Berries: Blueberries, strawberries, raspberries

- Whole fruits: Apples, pears, oranges

Dairy and Dairy Alternatives: Calcium for Health

Dairy products and their alternatives provide calcium, a mineral essential for bone health and metabolic function. Choose options that are low in added sugars and saturated fats:

- Low-fat or Greek yogurt

- Unsweetened almond milk, coconut milk, soy milk

Balancing Act: Combining Foods for Optimal Impact

The key to a prediabetes-friendly diet is balance. By skillfully combining complex carbohydrates, lean proteins, healthy fats, and fiber-rich foods, you can create meals that promote stable blood sugar levels and sustained energy throughout the day.

As you journey through this chapter, remember that the foods you select are not mere components of your meals – they are potent tools that can empower you to take control of your health. By incorporating these prediabetes-friendly foods into your dietary repertoire, you're forging a path toward improved well-being and a brighter, healthier future.

Chapter 5:

Foods to Limit or Avoid

In the intricate choreography of managing prediabetes, not all foods are created equal. Some can send blood sugar levels soaring, undermine insulin sensitivity, and hinder your progress toward optimal health. This chapter serves as your guide to recognizing and navigating the dietary pitfalls – a compass that directs you away from foods that can exacerbate prediabetes and toward a path of informed choices.

The Sugary Temptation: Unveiling Hidden Dangers

Sugar, the sweet siren that tantalizes taste buds, poses a significant threat to blood sugar stability. Foods high in added sugars contribute to rapid spikes and crashes in blood glucose levels, making their consumption particularly perilous for those managing prediabetes. Keep a vigilant eye on foods and beverages laden with sugars:

- Sugary beverages: Sodas, fruit juices, energy drinks

- Sweets: Candies, pastries, cookies, cakes

- Sweetened cereals

The Processed Predicament: Navigating a Minefield

Highly processed foods, often engineered for flavor and convenience, frequently harbor added sugars, unhealthy fats, and excessive salt. These culinary culprits not only disrupt blood sugar control but also contribute to inflammation and overall health issues. Exercise caution around:

- Processed snacks: Chips, crackers, packaged cookies

- Fast food: Burgers, fries, fried chicken

- Pre-packaged meals and frozen dinners

The Fat Fiasco: Treading Lightly on Fatty Ground

While fats are an essential part of a balanced diet, certain types can undermine your prediabetes management efforts. Trans fats and excessive saturated fats can contribute to insulin resistance and cardiovascular problems. Be mindful of:

- Trans fats: Found in many fried and commercially baked foods

- High-fat processed meats: Sausages, bacon, fatty cuts of beef

- Full-fat dairy products: Butter, full-fat cheese, cream

The Sodium Snare: Cutting Back on Salt

Excessive sodium intake can elevate blood pressure and contribute to heart health concerns, especially for individuals with prediabetes. Limit your consumption of high-sodium foods:

- Salty snacks: Potato chips, pretzels

- Processed meats: Cold cuts, deli meats

- Canned soups and ready-made sauces

Navigating Temptations: Strategies for Success

Recognizing foods to limit or avoid is the first step in crafting a prediabetes-friendly diet. However, complete avoidance isn't always feasible or enjoyable. Instead, practice moderation and apply strategies to manage cravings:

- Portion control: Enjoy treats in small portions on occasion.

- Read labels: Scrutinize nutrition labels for hidden sugars, unhealthy fats, and excessive sodium.

- Mindful eating: Savor each bite and eat with awareness to prevent overindulgence.

- Healthy swaps: Replace sugary or processed options with whole, nutrient-dense alternatives.

As you navigate the realm of foods to limit or avoid, remember that the goal isn't perfection but progress. By arming yourself with knowledge and cultivating mindful eating habits, you empower yourself to make choices that support your prediabetes management journey. Through informed decisions, you steer yourself away from dietary pitfalls and set a course toward improved well-being and vitality.

—

Chapter 6

Cookbook for prediabetes

Complex carbohydrates

1. Quinoa and Vegetable Stir-Fry:

A colorful medley of cooked quinoa, assorted vegetables like bell peppers, broccoli, and carrots, lightly sautéed with garlic and ginger. Quinoa provides a protein boost while the veggies add vitamins and minerals.

Ingredients:

- 1 cup quinoa, rinsed

- 2 cups mixed vegetables (bell peppers, broccoli, carrots), chopped

- 2 cloves garlic, minced

- 1 tsp fresh ginger, grated

- 2 tbsp low-sodium soy sauce

- 1 tbsp sesame oil

- Optional toppings: chopped green onions, sesame seeds

Instructions:

1. Cook quinoa according to package instructions.

2. In a large pan or wok, heat sesame oil over medium heat.

3. Add minced garlic and grated ginger, sauté for 1-2 minutes until fragrant.

4. Add mixed vegetables and stir-fry for about 5-7 minutes until tender-crisp.

5. Stir in cooked quinoa and soy sauce, tossing everything together.

6. Cook for an additional 2-3 minutes to heat through.

7. Serve hot, garnished with chopped green onions and sesame seeds if desired.

2. Brown Rice and Black Bean Burrito Bowl:

Nutrient-packed brown rice layered with black beans, salsa, avocado, and a sprinkle of cheese. This hearty dish is a great source of fiber, protein, and healthy fats.

Ingredients:

- 1 cup cooked brown rice

- 1 cup black beans, drained and rinsed

- 1/2 cup salsa

- 1 avocado, sliced

- 1/4 cup shredded cheese (cheddar, Monterey Jack, or vegan cheese)

- Fresh cilantro, chopped

Instructions:

1. In a serving bowl, layer cooked brown rice, black beans, and salsa.

2. Top with sliced avocado and shredded cheese.

3. Garnish with chopped cilantro.

4. Serve as a delicious and nutritious burrito bowl.

3. Oatmeal with Berries and Nuts:

   Creamy oats topped with a handful of fresh berries (such as blueberries or strawberries) and a mix of chopped nuts like almonds or walnuts. This breakfast dish is high in fiber, antioxidants, and heart-healthy fats.

Ingredients:

- 1 cup old-fashioned oats

- 2 cups water or milk (dairy or plant-based)

- 1 cup mixed berries (blueberries, strawberries, raspberries)

- 1/4 cup chopped nuts (almonds, walnuts, or your choice)

- Honey or maple syrup for sweetness (optional)

Instructions:

1. In a saucepan, bring water or milk to a boil.

2. Stir in oats and reduce heat to low. Cook for about 5 minutes, stirring occasionally.

3. Once the oats are cooked and creamy, remove from heat.

4. Top with mixed berries and chopped nuts.

5. Drizzle with honey or maple syrup if desired.

6. Enjoy a wholesome and filling breakfast.

4. Barley and Lentil Soup:

A warm and comforting soup made with cooked barley, lentils, diced vegetables, and aromatic herbs. Barley and lentils provide a combination of complex carbs and plant-based protein.

Ingredients:

- 1/2 cup barley, rinsed

- 1/2 cup dried green or brown lentils, rinsed

- 1 onion, chopped

- 2 carrots, peeled and chopped

- 2 celery stalks, chopped

- 2 cloves garlic, minced

- 6 cups vegetable or chicken broth

- 1 tsp dried thyme

- Salt and pepper to taste

- Fresh parsley, chopped (for garnish)

Instructions:

1. In a large pot, sauté chopped onion, carrots, and celery in a bit of olive oil until softened.

2. Add minced garlic and cook for another minute.

3. Add barley, lentils, thyme, and broth. Bring to a boil.

4. Reduce heat to a simmer, cover, and cook for about 25-30 minutes until barley and lentils are tender.

5. Season with salt and pepper to taste.

6. Serve hot, garnished with chopped fresh parsley.

5. Sweet Potato and Chickpea Curry:

A flavorful curry featuring chunks of sweet potato and tender chickpeas cooked in a fragrant blend of spices and coconut milk. Serve over brown rice for a well-rounded meal.

Ingredients:

- 2 large sweet potatoes, peeled and cubed

- 1 can (15 oz) chickpeas, drained and rinsed

- 1 onion, chopped

- 2 cloves garlic, minced

- 1 tbsp curry powder

- 1 tsp ground cumin

- 1 tsp ground coriander

- 1/2 tsp turmeric

- 1 can (14 oz) diced tomatoes

- 1 can (13.5 oz) coconut milk

- Salt and pepper to taste

- Fresh cilantro, chopped (for garnish)

Instructions:

1. In a large pot, sauté chopped onion in a bit of oil until translucent.

2. Add minced garlic and cook for another minute.

3. Stir in curry powder, cumin, coriander, and turmeric.

4. Add cubed sweet potatoes, chickpeas, diced tomatoes, and coconut milk. Stir well.

5. Bring to a simmer and let it cook for about 15-20 minutes until sweet potatoes are tender.

6. Season with salt and pepper to taste.

7. Serve the curry over cooked brown rice.

8. Garnish with chopped cilantro.

6. Whole Wheat Pasta Primavera:

Whole wheat pasta tossed with a variety of sautéed seasonal vegetables, such as zucchini, cherry tomatoes, and asparagus. This dish offers a wholesome twist on traditional pasta.

Ingredients:

- 8 oz whole wheat pasta

- 2 cups mixed vegetables (zucchini, cherry tomatoes, asparagus), chopped

- 2 cloves garlic, minced

- 2 tbsp olive oil

- 1/4 cup grated Parmesan cheese (optional)

- Fresh basil leaves, chopped

- Salt and pepper to taste

Instructions:

1. Cook whole wheat pasta according to package instructions.

2. In a large skillet, heat olive oil over medium heat.

3. Add minced garlic and sauté for about 1 minute until fragrant.

4. Add chopped vegetables and sauté until tender-crisp.

5. Toss cooked pasta with the sautéed vegetables.

6. Season with salt and pepper to taste.

7. Serve hot, garnished with grated Parmesan cheese and chopped fresh basil.

7. Farro and Roasted Vegetable Salad:

Nutty farro combined with roasted vegetables (like butternut squash, Brussels sprouts, and red onion), fresh herbs, and a light vinaigrette. Farro adds a chewy texture and a dose of fiber.

Ingredients:

- 1 cup farro, rinsed

- 2 cups mixed roasted vegetables (butternut squash, Brussels sprouts, red onion), cubed

- 1/4 cup feta cheese, crumbled

- 2 tbsp balsamic vinegar

- 2 tbsp olive oil

- Fresh parsley, chopped

- Salt and pepper to taste

Instructions:

1. Cook farro according to package instructions.

2. Toss cubed roasted vegetables with olive oil, salt, and pepper. Roast in the oven until tender.

3. In a large bowl, combine cooked farro, roasted vegetables, and crumbled feta cheese.

4. Drizzle with balsamic vinegar and olive oil.

5. Season with salt and pepper to taste.

6. Garnish with chopped fresh parsley.

7. Serve as a satisfying salad or side dish.

8. Millet Stuffed Bell Peppers:

Bell peppers filled with a mixture of cooked millet, lean ground turkey or tofu, diced tomatoes, and herbs. Baked until tender, this dish is a delightful source of whole grains and protein.

Ingredients:

- 4 large bell peppers, halved and seeds removed

- 1 cup cooked millet

- 1/2 lb lean ground turkey (or tofu for a vegetarian option)

- 1 cup diced tomatoes

- 1/2 cup onion, chopped

- 1/2 cup shredded cheese (cheddar or your choice)

- 1 tsp Italian seasoning

- Salt and pepper to taste

Instructions:

1. Preheat the oven to 375°F (190°C).

2. In a skillet, cook ground turkey (or crumbled tofu) until cooked through. Add chopped onion and cook until translucent.

3. Stir in cooked millet, diced tomatoes, Italian seasoning, salt, and pepper.

4. Fill each bell pepper half with the millet and turkey (or tofu) mixture.

5. Place stuffed peppers in a baking dish and cover with foil.

6. Bake for about 25-30 minutes until peppers are tender.

7. Remove foil, sprinkle shredded cheese on top, and bake for an additional 5 minutes until cheese is melted.

8. Serve the stuffed peppers as a hearty and flavorful main dish.

9. Buckwheat Pancakes with Fruit Compote:

Fluffy buckwheat pancakes topped with a homemade fruit compote made from mixed berries, a touch of honey, and a squeeze of lemon. Buckwheat flour offers a gluten-free complex carbohydrate option.

Ingredients:

- 1 cup buckwheat flour

- 1 tsp baking powder

- 1/2 tsp cinnamon

- 1 cup almond milk (or any milk of your choice)

- 1 egg (or flax egg for a vegan option)

- 1 tbsp maple syrup

- For the fruit compote:

- 1 cup mixed berries (blueberries, strawberries, raspberries)

- 2 tbsp honey or maple syrup

- 1 tbsp lemon juice

Instructions:

1. In a mixing bowl, whisk together buckwheat flour, baking powder, and cinnamon.

2. In a separate bowl, whisk together almond milk, egg, and maple syrup.

3. Combine wet and dry ingredients and stir until just combined.

4. Heat a non-stick skillet over medium heat. Pour 1/4 cup of batter onto the skillet for each pancake.

5. Cook until bubbles form on the surface, then flip and cook for another 1-2 minutes until golden brown.

6. For the fruit compote, combine mixed berries, honey or maple syrup, and lemon juice in a small saucepan. Cook over medium heat until the berries break down and the mixture thickens.

7. Serve the buckwheat pancakes topped with the fruit compote.

10. Couscous Salad with Mediterranean Flavors:

A light and refreshing couscous salad featuring cooked couscous, chopped cucumber, tomatoes, Kalamata olives, feta cheese, and a drizzle of olive oil and lemon juice. Perfect for a quick and satisfying lunch.

Ingredients:

- 1 cup couscous

- 1 1/2 cups water or vegetable broth

- 1 cucumber, diced

- 1 cup cherry tomatoes, halved

- 1/2 cup Kalamata olives, pitted and sliced

- 1/4 cup crumbled feta cheese

- 2 tbsp olive oil

- 2 tbsp lemon juice

- Fresh parsley, chopped

- Salt and pepper to taste

Instructions:

1. In a saucepan, bring water or vegetable broth to a boil. Stir in couscous, cover, and remove from heat. Let it sit for 5 minutes, then fluff with a fork.

2. In a large bowl, combine cooked couscous, diced cucumber, halved cherry tomatoes, sliced Kalamata olives, and crumbled feta cheese.

3. Drizzle with olive oil and lemon juice. Toss to combine.

4. Season with salt and pepper to taste.

5. Garnish with chopped fresh parsley.

6. Serve the couscous salad as a refreshing and satisfying side dish.

Lean proteins

1. Grilled Chicken Breast with Quinoa Salad:

Grilled boneless, skinless chicken breast served with a refreshing quinoa salad featuring diced cucumbers, cherry tomatoes, red onion, and fresh herbs. A light vinaigrette enhances the flavors, creating a balanced and protein-packed meal.

Ingredients:

- 2 boneless, skinless chicken breasts

- 1 cup quinoa, rinsed

- 1 1/2 cups water or chicken broth

- 1 cucumber, diced

- 1 cup cherry tomatoes, halved

- 1/4 red onion, finely chopped

- Fresh parsley and mint, chopped

- 3 tbsp olive oil

- 2 tbsp lemon juice

- Salt and pepper to taste

Instructions:

1. Preheat the grill to medium-high heat.

2. Season chicken breasts with salt and pepper. Grill for about 6-7 minutes per side, or until fully cooked.

3. In a saucepan, bring water or chicken broth to a boil. Stir in quinoa, cover, and let simmer for 15-20 minutes until cooked.

4. In a large bowl, combine cooked quinoa, diced cucumber, halved cherry tomatoes, chopped red onion, and fresh herbs.

5. Whisk together olive oil, lemon juice, salt, and pepper. Drizzle over the quinoa salad and toss to combine.

6. Serve the grilled chicken over the quinoa salad.

2. Baked Salmon with Steamed Asparagus:

Succulent salmon fillet seasoned and baked to perfection, accompanied by tender steamed asparagus spears. The dish is rich in omega-3 fatty acids and provides a satisfying protein boost.

Ingredients:

- 2 salmon fillets

- 1 bunch asparagus, trimmed

- 2 tbsp olive oil

- Lemon slices

- Fresh dill, chopped

- Salt and pepper to taste

Instructions:

1. Preheat the oven to 375°F (190°C).

2. Place salmon fillets on a baking sheet. Drizzle with olive oil and season with salt, pepper, and chopped dill. Top with lemon slices.

3. Bake for about 15-20 minutes, or until salmon flakes easily with a fork.

4. Steam asparagus for 4-5 minutes until tender.

5. Serve the baked salmon alongside steamed asparagus.

3. Tofu and Vegetable Stir-Fry:

Cubes of firm tofu sautéed with an array of colorful vegetables (bell peppers, broccoli, snap peas) in a savory ginger and garlic sauce. This plant-based dish is a delightful source of protein and essential nutrients.

Ingredients:

- 1 block firm tofu, pressed and cubed

- 2 cups mixed vegetables (bell peppers, broccoli, snap peas), sliced

- 2 tbsp low-sodium soy sauce

- 1 tbsp sesame oil

- 2 cloves garlic, minced

- 1 tsp fresh ginger, grated

- Optional toppings: sliced green onions, sesame seeds

Instructions:

1. In a large pan or wok, heat sesame oil over medium heat.

2. Add minced garlic and grated ginger, sauté for 1-2 minutes until fragrant.

3. Add cubed tofu and stir-fry until lightly browned.

4. Add sliced vegetables and continue to stir-fry for about 5-7 minutes until tender-crisp.

5. Stir in low-sodium soy sauce and toss to coat.

6. Cook for an additional 2-3 minutes to heat through.

7. Serve the tofu and vegetable stir-fry hot, garnished with sliced green onions and sesame seeds.

4. Turkey and Black Bean Chili:

Ground turkey simmered with black beans, diced tomatoes, onions, and a medley of spices to create a hearty and flavorful chili. This protein-packed comfort food is perfect for chilly evenings.

Ingredients:

- 1 lb ground turkey

- 1 onion, chopped

- 2 cloves garlic, minced

- 1 can (15 oz) black beans, drained and rinsed

- 1 can (14 oz) diced tomatoes

- 1 cup low-sodium chicken broth

- 2 tbsp chili powder

- 1 tsp ground cumin

- 1/2 tsp paprika

- Salt and pepper to taste

- Optional toppings: chopped cilantro, Greek yogurt, shredded cheese

Instructions:

1. In a large pot, sauté chopped onion and ground turkey until turkey is cooked through and no longer pink.

2. Add minced garlic, chili powder, cumin, paprika, salt, and pepper. Cook for another 1-2 minutes.

3. Add black beans, diced tomatoes, and chicken broth. Stir well.

4. Simmer for about 20-25 minutes, allowing the flavors to meld.

5. Serve the turkey and black bean chili hot, with your choice of optional toppings.

5. Greek Yogurt Parfait with Berries and Nuts:

Creamy Greek yogurt layered with a mix of fresh berries (blueberries, raspberries) and chopped nuts (almonds, walnuts). A drizzle of honey adds sweetness to this protein-rich breakfast or snack.

Ingredients:

- 1 cup Greek yogurt

- 1/2 cup mixed berries (blueberries, raspberries)

- 2 tbsp chopped nuts (almonds, walnuts)

- 1 tbsp honey or maple syrup (optional)

Instructions:

1. In a glass or bowl, layer Greek yogurt, mixed berries, and chopped nuts.

2. Drizzle with honey or maple syrup if desired.

3. Serve the Greek yogurt parfait as a protein-rich breakfast or snack.

6. Egg White Veggie Omelette:

Fluffy egg white omelette filled with sautéed spinach, tomatoes, onions, and a sprinkle of low-fat cheese. This low-calorie, high-protein dish is a great way to start your day.

Ingredients:

- 4 egg whites

- 1/4 cup diced tomatoes

- 1/4 cup chopped spinach

- 1/4 cup diced onions

- 2 tbsp low-fat shredded cheese

- Salt and pepper to taste

- Cooking spray or a touch of olive oil

Instructions:

1. In a bowl, whisk egg whites with a pinch of salt and pepper.

2. Heat a non-stick skillet over medium heat. Lightly coat with cooking spray or olive oil.

3. Pour the egg whites into the skillet and let them cook for a minute.

4. Sprinkle diced tomatoes, chopped spinach, and diced onions over one half of the eggs.

5. Sprinkle shredded cheese over the vegetables.

6. Fold the other half of the omelette over the vegetables and cheese.

7. Cook for another 2-3 minutes until the omelette is cooked through and cheese is melted.

8. Slide the omelette onto a plate and serve.

7. Lentil and Spinach Salad with Grilled Shrimp:

Nutrient-packed lentils and fresh spinach combined with succulent grilled shrimp. A zesty lemon vinaigrette ties the flavors together in this protein-rich salad.

Ingredients:

- 1 cup cooked green or brown lentils

- 2 cups fresh spinach leaves

- 1/2 lb large shrimp, peeled and deveined

- 1 lemon, zest and juice

- 2 tbsp olive oil

- 1 clove garlic, minced

- Salt and pepper to taste

Instructions:

1. In a bowl, combine cooked lentils, fresh spinach, lemon zest, and juice.

2. In a separate bowl, whisk together olive oil, minced garlic, salt, and pepper.

3. Toss half of the dressing with the lentil and spinach mixture.

4. Season shrimp with salt and pepper. Grill or sauté until cooked through.

5. Drizzle the remaining dressing over the cooked shrimp.

6. Serve the lentil and spinach salad topped with grilled shrimp.

8. White Bean and Chicken Salad:

A refreshing salad featuring shredded cooked chicken, white beans, chopped celery, red onion, and a light yogurt-based dressing. Packed with lean protein and fiber, this salad makes for a satisfying lunch.

Ingredients:

- 2 cups cooked shredded chicken breast

- 1 can (15 oz) white beans, drained and rinsed

- 1 cup diced celery

- 1/2 cup diced red onion

- 1/4 cup plain Greek yogurt

- 1 tbsp Dijon mustard

- 2 tbsp lemon juice

- Salt and pepper to taste

Instructions:

1. In a bowl, combine shredded chicken, white beans, diced celery, and diced red onion.

2. In a separate bowl, whisk together Greek yogurt, Dijon mustard, lemon juice, salt, and pepper.

3. Toss the dressing with the chicken and bean mixture until well coated.

4. Serve the white bean and chicken salad as a wholesome lunch.

9. Seared Tuna Steak with Avocado Salsa:

Sear-crisped tuna steak topped with a vibrant salsa made from ripe avocados, diced tomatoes, red onion, and cilantro. This dish is a harmonious fusion of protein and healthy fats.

Ingredients:

- 2 tuna steaks

- 1 ripe avocado, diced

- 1 cup diced tomatoes

- 1/4 cup red onion, finely chopped

- 2 tbsp chopped cilantro

- 1 lime, zest and juice

- Salt and pepper to taste

Instructions:

1. Season tuna steaks with salt and pepper.

2. Heat a skillet or grill pan over high heat. Sear the tuna steaks for about 2-3 minutes per side for medium-rare.

3. In a bowl, combine diced avocado, diced tomatoes, chopped red onion, chopped cilantro, lime zest, and juice.

4. Season the avocado salsa with salt and pepper.

5. Serve the seared tuna steaks with a generous spoonful of avocado salsa on top.

10. Lean Beef Stir-Fry with Broccoli:

Slices of lean beef stir-fried with crisp broccoli florets in a soy-ginger sauce. This protein-rich dish is a savory and satisfying option for those seeking a balance of flavors and nutrients.

Ingredients:

- 1/2 lb lean beef (such as sirloin), thinly sliced

- 2 cups broccoli florets

- 2 tbsp low-sodium soy sauce

- 1 tbsp hoisin sauce

- 1 tsp cornstarch

- 2 cloves garlic, minced

- 1 tsp fresh ginger, grated

- 1 tbsp vegetable oil

- Optional toppings: sliced green onions, sesame seeds

Instructions:

1. In a bowl, whisk together soy sauce, hoisin sauce, and cornstarch. Set aside.

2. Heat vegetable oil in a skillet or wok over high heat.

3. Add minced garlic and grated ginger, sauté for 1-2 minutes until fragrant.

4. Add thinly sliced beef and stir-fry until cooked. Remove from the skillet.

5. In the same skillet, stir-fry broccoli florets until tender-crisp.

6. Return the cooked beef to the skillet and pour the sauce over the ingredients.

7. Toss everything together until well coated and heated through.

8. Serve the beef stir-fry hot, garnished with sliced green onions and sesame seeds.

Healthy fats

1. Avocado Toast with Poached Egg:

Creamy avocado spread on whole-grain toast, topped with a perfectly poached egg. Avocado provides heart-healthy monounsaturated fats, while the egg adds a protein boost.

Ingredients:

- 2 slices whole-grain bread, toasted

- 1 ripe avocado, mashed

- 2 large eggs

- Salt and pepper to taste

- Optional toppings: red pepper flakes, chopped fresh herbs

Instructions:

1. Toast the whole-grain bread slices.

2. While the bread is toasting, poach the eggs in simmering water for about 3-4 minutes until the whites are set but the yolks are still runny.

3. Spread mashed avocado evenly on the toasted bread slices.

4. Place a poached egg on top of each slice.

5. Season with salt and pepper, and sprinkle with optional toppings.

6. Serve the avocado toast with poached egg for a nutritious breakfast or brunch.

2. Salmon Salad with Mixed Greens and Walnuts:

Flaked salmon served on a bed of mixed greens, cherry tomatoes, cucumber, and topped with crunchy walnuts. The salmon offers omega-3 fatty acids, while walnuts provide additional healthy fats and texture.

Ingredients:

- 2 salmon fillets, cooked and flaked

- 4 cups mixed salad greens

- 1 cup cherry tomatoes, halved

- 1 cucumber, sliced

- 1/2 cup chopped walnuts

- Olive oil and balsamic vinegar for dressing

- Salt and pepper to taste

Instructions:

1. In a large bowl, combine mixed salad greens, cherry tomatoes, cucumber, and chopped walnuts.

2. Drizzle olive oil and balsamic vinegar over the salad, and toss to coat.

3. Gently fold in the flaked salmon.

4. Season with salt and pepper to taste.

5. Serve the salmon salad with mixed greens and walnuts as a satisfying and nutrient-rich meal.

3. Greek Yogurt Parfait with Nut Butter:

Creamy Greek yogurt layered with your favorite nut butter, a drizzle of honey, and a sprinkle of granola. Nut butter adds a dose of healthy fats and protein to this satisfying breakfast or snack.

Ingredients:

- 1 cup Greek yogurt

- 2 tbsp nut butter (almond, peanut, or your choice)

- 1 tbsp honey or maple syrup

- 1/4 cup granola

- Fresh berries for topping

Instructions:

1. In a serving glass or bowl, layer Greek yogurt, nut butter, and honey or maple syrup.

2. Sprinkle granola over the yogurt and nut butter layers.

3. Top with fresh berries.

4. Enjoy the Greek yogurt parfait with nut butter as a delicious and protein-packed breakfast or snack.

4. Quinoa and Avocado Stuffed Bell Peppers:

Bell peppers filled with a mixture of cooked quinoa, diced avocado, black beans, corn, and a squeeze of lime. Avocado contributes rich, nourishing fats to this colorful and nutritious dish.

Ingredients:

- 2 large bell peppers, halved and seeds removed

- 1 cup cooked quinoa

- 1 avocado, diced

- 1/2 cup black beans, drained and rinsed

- 1/4 cup corn kernels (fresh, frozen, or canned)

- Juice of 1 lime

- Fresh cilantro, chopped

- Salt and pepper to taste

Instructions:

1. Preheat the oven to 375°F (190°C).

2. In a bowl, combine cooked quinoa, diced avocado, black beans, corn, lime juice, and chopped cilantro.

3. Season with salt and pepper to taste.

4. Fill each bell pepper half with the quinoa and avocado mixture.

5. Place stuffed peppers in a baking dish and cover with foil.

6. Bake for about 25-30 minutes until peppers are tender.

7. Serve the quinoa and avocado stuffed bell peppers as a wholesome and flavorful meal.

5. Olive Oil and Herb Marinated Chicken Skewers:

Chicken skewers marinated in a blend of olive oil, fresh herbs, garlic, and lemon juice. The healthy fats in olive oil infuse flavor and tenderness into the grilled chicken.

Ingredients:

- 1 lb boneless, skinless chicken breasts, cut into cubes

- 1/4 cup olive oil

- 2 cloves garlic, minced

- 1 tbsp fresh herbs (such as rosemary, thyme, or oregano), chopped

- Juice of 1 lemon

- Salt and pepper to taste

Instructions:

1. In a bowl, whisk together olive oil, minced garlic, chopped fresh herbs, lemon juice, salt, and pepper.

2. Add the chicken cubes to the marinade and toss to coat. Let marinate for at least 30 minutes.

3. Preheat the grill or grill pan over medium-high heat.

4. Thread the marinated chicken cubes onto skewers.

5. Grill the chicken skewers for about 5-6 minutes per side, or until fully cooked and slightly charred.

6. Serve the olive oil and herb marinated chicken skewers as a flavorful and protein-rich dish.

6. Coconut Curry Lentil Soup:

A hearty lentil soup made with red lentils, coconut milk, and a fragrant blend of curry spices. Coconut milk adds a velvety texture and healthy coconut fats to this comforting dish.

Ingredients:

- 1 cup red lentils, rinsed and drained

- 1 can (14 oz) coconut milk

- 4 cups vegetable broth

- 1 onion, chopped

- 2 cloves garlic, minced

- 1 tbsp curry powder

- 1 tsp ground cumin

- 1 tsp ground turmeric

- 1 tsp grated ginger

- 2 tbsp olive oil

- Salt and pepper to taste

- Fresh cilantro, chopped (for garnish)

Instructions:

1. In a large pot, heat olive oil over medium heat. Add chopped onion and sauté until translucent.

2. Add minced garlic, curry powder, cumin, turmeric, and grated ginger. Cook for another minute.

3. Add red lentils, coconut milk, and vegetable broth. Stir well.

4. Bring to a boil, then reduce heat to a simmer. Cover and cook for about 20-25 minutes, or until lentils are tender.

5. Season with salt and pepper to taste.

6. Serve the coconut curry lentil soup hot, garnished with chopped fresh cilantro.

7. Mixed Berry and Almond Smoothie Bowl:

A thick and creamy smoothie bowl featuring mixed berries, almond milk, and a sprinkle of sliced almonds. Almonds provide healthy fats, while the berries add antioxidants and natural sweetness.

Ingredients:

- 1 cup mixed berries (blueberries, strawberries, raspberries)

- 1/2 cup almond milk (or any milk of your choice)

- 1 banana, frozen

- 2 tbsp almond butter

- Toppings: sliced almonds, chia seeds, shredded coconut, fresh berries

Instructions:

1. In a blender, combine mixed berries, almond milk, frozen banana, and almond butter.

2. Blend until smooth and creamy.

3. Pour the smoothie into a bowl.

4. Top with sliced almonds, chia seeds, shredded coconut, and fresh berries.

5. Enjoy the mixed berry and almond smoothie bowl as a nutrient-packed breakfast or snack.

8. Hummus and Veggie Wrap with Avocado:

A whole-grain wrap filled with hummus, an assortment of fresh vegetables (spinach, bell peppers, cucumbers), and creamy avocado slices. Avocado lends a luscious texture and beneficial fats.

Ingredients:

- 1 whole-grain wrap or tortilla

- 1/4 cup hummus

- 1/2 avocado, sliced

- Assorted fresh vegetables (spinach, bell peppers, cucumber, carrots), sliced

- Salt and pepper to taste

Instructions:

1. Lay the whole-grain wrap flat.

2. Spread hummus evenly over the wrap.

3. Layer avocado slices and sliced fresh vegetables on top.

4. Season with salt and pepper to taste.

5. Roll up the wrap tightly, folding in the sides as you go.

6. Slice the wrap in half and enjoy the hummus and veggie wrap with avocado.

9. Spinach and Feta Stuffed Mushrooms:

Mushrooms stuffed with a mixture of sautéed spinach, crumbled feta cheese, garlic, and a touch of olive oil. Feta cheese and olive oil bring a savory richness to this appetizer or side dish.

Ingredients:

- 12 large mushrooms, stems removed

- 2 cups baby spinach, chopped

- 1/2 cup crumbled feta cheese

- 2 cloves garlic, minced

- 2 tbsp olive oil

- Salt and pepper to taste

Instructions:

1. Preheat the oven to 375°F (190°C).

2. In a skillet, heat olive oil over medium heat. Add minced garlic and sauté for 1-2 minutes until fragrant.

3. Add chopped baby spinach and sauté until wilted.

4. Remove from heat and stir in crumbled feta cheese.

5. Stuff each mushroom cap with the spinach and feta mixture.

6. Place stuffed mushrooms on a baking sheet.

7. Bake for about 15-20 minutes until mushrooms are tender.

8. Serve the spinach and feta stuffed mushrooms as a flavorful appetizer or side dish.

10. Dark Chocolate-Dipped Strawberries:

Fresh strawberries dipped in melted dark chocolate and sprinkled with crushed nuts or coconut flakes. Dark chocolate contains antioxidants and healthy fats, making this dessert a delightful treat.

Ingredients:

- Fresh strawberries, washed and dried

- Dark chocolate (70% cocoa or higher), chopped

- Crushed nuts (almonds, pistachios, etc.) or shredded coconut (optional)

Instructions:

1. Melt the dark chocolate using a double boiler or microwave in short intervals, stirring until smooth.

2. Hold each strawberry by the stem and dip it into the melted chocolate, covering about two-thirds of the strawberry.

3. Allow any excess chocolate to drip off before placing the dipped strawberry on a parchment-lined tray.

4. If desired, sprinkle crushed nuts or shredded coconut over the chocolate-dipped strawberries while the chocolate is still wet.

5. Place the tray in the refrigerator for the chocolate to set.

6. Once the chocolate is firm, remove the strawberries from the refrigerator and enjoy the dark chocolate-dipped strawberries as a delightful and healthier dessert.

High fiber meals

1. Oatmeal with Berries and Nuts:

   Creamy oatmeal topped with a generous serving of mixed berries (blueberries, strawberries, raspberries) and a sprinkle of chopped nuts (almonds, walnuts). This fiber-rich breakfast provides a warm and satisfying start to the day.

Ingredients:

- 1 cup rolled oats

- 2 cups water or milk (dairy or plant-based)

- 1 cup mixed berries (blueberries, strawberries, raspberries)

- 1/4 cup chopped nuts (almonds, walnuts)

- 1 tbsp honey or maple syrup (optional)

Instructions:

1. In a saucepan, bring water or milk to a boil.

2. Stir in rolled oats and reduce heat to a simmer.

3. Cook for about 5 minutes, stirring occasionally, until the oatmeal reaches your desired consistency.

4. Divide the oatmeal into serving bowls.

5. Top with mixed berries, chopped nuts, and a drizzle of honey or maple syrup if desired.

6. Serve the oatmeal with berries and nuts for a hearty and fiber-rich breakfast.

2. Chickpea and Vegetable Stir-Fry:

A flavorful stir-fry featuring chickpeas, colorful bell peppers, broccoli, and snap peas, all sautéed in a ginger-garlic sauce. Serve over brown rice for a high-fiber and plant-based meal.

Ingredients:

- 1 can (15 oz) chickpeas, drained and rinsed

- 2 cups mixed vegetables (bell peppers, broccoli, snap peas), sliced

- 2 tbsp low-sodium soy sauce

- 1 tbsp sesame oil

- 2 cloves garlic, minced

- 1 tsp fresh ginger, grated

- Cooked brown rice for serving

Instructions:

1. In a large pan or wok, heat sesame oil over medium heat.

2. Add minced garlic and grated ginger, sauté for 1-2 minutes until fragrant.

3. Add sliced vegetables and sauté for about 5-7 minutes until tender-crisp.

4. Add chickpeas and low-sodium soy sauce. Toss to combine and heat through.

5. Serve the chickpea and vegetable stir-fry over cooked brown rice.

3. Black Bean and Quinoa Salad:

Nutrient-packed black beans and quinoa combined with diced tomatoes, red onion, cilantro, and a zesty lime vinaigrette. This hearty salad offers a delightful blend of flavors and a substantial dose of fiber.

Ingredients:

- 1 cup cooked quinoa

- 1 can (15 oz) black beans, drained and rinsed

- 1 cup diced tomatoes

- 1/4 cup red onion, finely chopped

- 1/4 cup fresh cilantro, chopped

- Juice of 1 lime

- 2 tbsp olive oil

- Salt and pepper to taste

Instructions:

1. In a large bowl, combine cooked quinoa, black beans, diced tomatoes, red onion, and chopped cilantro.

2. In a separate bowl, whisk together lime juice, olive oil, salt, and pepper.

3. Pour the dressing over the quinoa mixture and toss to combine.

4. Serve the black bean and quinoa salad as a fiber-rich and refreshing side dish.

4. Whole Wheat Pasta Primavera:

  Whole wheat pasta tossed with a medley of fresh spring vegetables (zucchini, cherry tomatoes, asparagus) and a light olive oil and herb dressing. This high-fiber pasta dish is both colorful and nourishing.

Ingredients:

- 8 oz whole wheat pasta (such as penne or spaghetti)

- 2 cups mixed vegetables (zucchini, cherry tomatoes, asparagus), sliced

- 2 cloves garlic, minced

- 2 tbsp olive oil

- 1 tbsp fresh basil, chopped

- Salt and pepper to taste

- Grated Parmesan cheese (optional)

Instructions:

1. Cook the whole wheat pasta according to package instructions. Drain and set aside.

2. In a large skillet, heat olive oil over medium heat.

3. Add minced garlic and sauté for about 1 minute until fragrant.

4. Add sliced vegetables and sauté for 5-7 minutes until tender.

5. Toss the cooked pasta and chopped basil with the sautéed vegetables.

6. Season with salt and pepper to taste.

7. Serve the whole wheat pasta primavera with a sprinkle of grated Parmesan cheese if desired.

5. Lentil and Vegetable Curry:

A comforting curry made with red lentils, a variety of vegetables (carrots, spinach, cauliflower), and aromatic spices. Serve over brown rice or whole wheat naan for a fiber-packed meal.

Ingredients:

- 1 cup red lentils, rinsed and drained

- 2 cups mixed vegetables (carrots, spinach, cauliflower), chopped

- 1 can (14 oz) diced tomatoes

- 1 can (14 oz) coconut milk

- 2 tbsp curry powder

- 1 tsp ground cumin

- 1 tsp ground turmeric

- 1 tsp grated ginger

- 2 cloves garlic, minced

- 2 tbsp olive oil

- Salt and pepper to taste

- Cooked brown rice for serving

Instructions:

1. In a large pot, heat olive oil over medium heat.

2. Add minced garlic and grated ginger, sauté for 1-2 minutes until fragrant.

3. Add curry powder, cumin, turmeric, salt, and pepper. Cook for another minute.

4. Add mixed vegetables, diced tomatoes (with juices), and coconut milk. Stir well.

5. Bring to a boil, then reduce heat to a simmer. Cover and cook for about 20-25 minutes.

6. Add red lentils and continue to cook for an additional 15-20 minutes until lentils are tender.

7. Serve the lentil and vegetable curry over cooked brown rice.

6. Bean and Vegetable Soup:

Hearty soup brimming with various beans (kidney beans, cannellini beans, black beans) and an assortment of vegetables in a flavorful broth. This fiber-rich soup makes for a filling and comforting option.

Ingredients:

- 1 can (15 oz) mixed beans (kidney beans, cannellini beans, black beans), drained and rinsed

- 2 cups mixed vegetables (carrots, celery, onions), chopped

- 4 cups low-sodium vegetable broth

- 1 can (14 oz) diced tomatoes

- 2 cloves garlic, minced

- 1 tsp dried thyme

- Salt and pepper to taste

- Fresh parsley, chopped (for garnish)

Instructions:

1. In a large pot, sauté chopped vegetables and minced garlic until slightly softened.

2. Add mixed beans, diced tomatoes (with juices), vegetable broth, dried thyme, salt, and pepper. Stir well.

3. Bring to a boil, then reduce heat to a simmer. Cover and cook for about 20-25 minutes.

4. Serve the bean and vegetable soup hot, garnished with chopped fresh parsley.

7. Roasted Sweet Potato and Quinoa Bowl:

Roasted sweet potato cubes paired with cooked quinoa, sautéed greens, and a dollop of hummus. The combination of flavors and textures creates a satisfying and fiber-filled bowl.

Ingredients:

- 2 medium sweet potatoes, peeled and cubed

- 1 cup cooked quinoa

- 2 cups mixed greens (spinach, kale, arugula), chopped

- 1/4 cup hummus

- 1/4 cup pumpkin seeds

- Olive oil for roasting

- Salt and pepper to taste

Instructions:

1. Preheat the oven to 400°F (200°C).

2. Toss sweet potato cubes with olive oil, salt, and pepper. Spread on a baking sheet and roast for about 25-30 minutes, or until tender and golden.

3. In a bowl, layer cooked quinoa, roasted sweet potatoes, and mixed greens.

4. Dollop hummus on top and sprinkle with pumpkin seeds.

5. Serve the roasted sweet potato and quinoa bowl for a nourishing and filling meal.

8. High-Fiber Veggie Wrap:

   A whole-grain wrap filled with hummus, sliced avocado, grated carrots, mixed greens, and a sprinkle of chia seeds. This portable meal is a convenient way to enjoy a fiber-rich lunch on the go.

Ingredients:

- 1 whole-grain wrap or tortilla

- 1/4 cup hummus

- 1/2 avocado, sliced

- 1/2 cup grated carrots

- 1 cup mixed greens

- 1 tbsp chia seeds

- Salt and pepper to taste

Instructions:

1. Lay the whole-grain wrap flat.

2. Spread hummus evenly over the wrap.

3. Layer avocado slices, grated carrots, and mixed greens on top.

4. Sprinkle chia seeds over the vegetables.

5. Roll up the wrap tightly, folding in the sides as you go.

6. Slice the wrap in half and enjoy the high-fiber veggie wrap.

9. Fruit and Yogurt Parfait with Chia Seeds:

Layers of Greek yogurt, mixed fresh fruits (kiwi, pineapple, mango), and chia seeds. Chia seeds add an extra boost of fiber and omega-3 fatty acids to this nutritious parfait.

Ingredients:

- 1 cup Greek yogurt

- 1 cup mixed fresh fruits (kiwi, pineapple, mango), diced

- 2 tbsp chia seeds

- 1 tbsp honey or maple syrup (optional)

Instructions:

1. In a glass or bowl, layer Greek yogurt, mixed fresh fruits, and chia seeds.

2. Drizzle with honey or maple syrup if desired.

3. Serve the fruit and yogurt parfait with chia seeds as a wholesome and fiber-rich breakfast or snack.

10. Grilled Chicken and Quinoa Stuffed Bell Peppers:

   Bell peppers stuffed with a mixture of cooked quinoa, diced grilled chicken, black beans, corn, and a touch of salsa. These stuffed peppers provide a satisfying blend of protein and fiber.

Ingredients:

- 4 large bell peppers, halved and seeds removed

- 2 cups cooked quinoa

- 1 cup cooked diced chicken breast

- 1 can (15 oz) black beans, drained and rinsed

- 1/2 cup corn kernels (fresh, frozen, or canned)

- 1/2 cup salsa

- 1/2 cup shredded cheddar cheese (optional)

- Salt and pepper to taste

Instructions:

1. Preheat the oven to 375°F (190°C).

2. In a bowl, combine cooked quinoa, diced chicken, black beans, corn, and salsa.

3. Season with salt and pepper to taste.

4. Fill each bell pepper half with the quinoa and chicken mixture.

5. Place stuffed peppers in a baking dish. If using cheese, sprinkle shredded cheddar on top.

6. Cover with foil and bake for about 25-30 minutes until peppers are tender.

7. Serve the grilled chicken and quinoa stuffed bell peppers as a wholesome and satisfying meal.

Conclusion

In conclusion, "Food List for Prediabetes" aims to provide you with a comprehensive guide to making informed dietary choices that support your journey towards better health. Throughout this book, we have explored the concept of prediabetes, its risk factors, and the crucial role that diet plays in managing and preventing its progression. By understanding the power of balanced nutrition and the impact of various food choices, you've gained the tools to take charge of your health and make positive changes.

From learning about the benefits of complex carbohydrates and their role in maintaining stable blood sugar levels, to discovering the significance of lean proteins and healthy fats in supporting overall wellness, you've been equipped with valuable insights to curate a prediabetes-friendly menu. The inclusion of delicious and nutritious recipes, ranging from high-fiber meals to dishes rich in lean proteins and healthy fats, serves as a practical extension of the knowledge gained from these chapters.

By implementing the principles outlined in this book, you can embark on a journey of improved well-being and enhanced vitality. Remember, the road to better health is marked by progress, not perfection. Small changes can yield significant results over time, and every step towards healthier eating contributes to your long-term success in managing prediabetes and maintaining optimal health.

As you explore the recipes included in this book, experiment with flavors, embrace variety, and make each meal a celebration of nourishment. The recipes offer a rich tapestry of tastes, textures, and nutrients that align with the principles of prediabetes management. Whether you're savoring a bowl of fiber-rich black bean and quinoa salad, indulging in the wholesome goodness of grilled chicken and quinoa stuffed bell peppers, or treating yourself to the decadence of dark chocolate-dipped strawberries, each dish is crafted with your well-being in mind.

In closing, "Food List for Prediabetes" empowers you to take control of your health through mindful food choices, balanced nutrition, and a commitment to long-term wellness. Remember that your dietary journey is uniquely yours, and as you embark on this path, you're making a positive investment in your future. With the insights gained from this book and the delectable recipes at your fingertips, you have the tools to create a prediabetes-friendly food journey that supports your health, happiness, and vitality.

Here's to a vibrant life filled with delicious, nourishing meals and the empowerment that comes from informed choices. May your journey towards balanced nutrition be both gratifying and transformative, as you embark on a path of well-being and resilience against prediabetes.

About the author

Jerry V. Hatcher is a culinary virtuoso and the creative mind behind a collection of exquisite cookbooks that transcend the ordinary. With a passion for gastronomy and a flair for culinary artistry, Jerry has crafted a series of cookbooks that take readers on a delectable journey through the world of flavors.

Through his cookbooks, Jerry V. Hatcher combines the finest ingredients with meticulous instructions, ensuring every recipe is a delightful masterpiece waiting to be savored. From tantalizing appetizers to mouthwatering main courses and divine desserts, each page is a celebration of culinary excellence.

With a keen eye for detail, Jerry's cookbooks go beyond the recipes, providing valuable tips, techniques, and personal insights that elevate the cooking experience to new heights. Whether you're a seasoned chef or a culinary enthusiast exploring the kitchen for the first time, Jerry's books cater to all skill levels, fostering confidence and creativity in every home cook.

Each recipe in Jerry V. Hatcher's cookbooks is a reflection of his commitment to authenticity and a passion for diverse cuisines. Drawing inspiration from global flavors and local delicacies, Jerry's culinary creations celebrate the richness of cultures and the joy of sharing food with loved ones. Indulge your passion for cooking and elevate your culinary skills with the culinary masterpieces crafted by Jerry V. Hatcher. Get ready to embark on a gastronomic adventure that will leave you hungry for more, one delicious recipe at a time.

My Little Request

If you have gotten to this point, chances are high you have finished this book.

Thank You for Reading My Book!

I love hearing what you have to say.

I need your input to make the next version of this

book and my future books better.

Please take two minutes now to leave a helpful review on Amazon letting me know what you thought of the book

Thanks so much!

- Jerry V. Hatcher

Printed in Dunstable, United Kingdom